# HIKING

OUTDOOR ADVENTURES

## DAVID ARMENTROUT

The Rourke Press, Inc.
Vero Beach, Florida 32964

David Armentrout specializes in nonfiction writing and has had several
book series published for primary schools. He resides in Cincinnati with
his wife and two children.

PHOTO CREDITS
© Ace Kvale: cover, page 21: © Corel Corporation: page 4;
© International Stock: page 7; © Gordon Wiltsie: pages 9, 12, 13, 15, 19;
© Buddy Mays/International Stock: page 16; © Micheal Philip
Manheim/International Stock: page 18; © East Coast Studios: pages 6,
10, 22

EDITORIAL SERVICES:
Penworthy Learning Systems

**Library of Congress Cataloging-in-Publication Data**

Armentrout, David, 1962-
    Hiking / David Armentrout.
       p.  cm. — (Outdoor adventures)
    Includes bibliographical references (p.24) and index.
    Summary: An introduction to hiking, covering such aspects as planning,
clothing, supplies, food, safety, and the enjoyment of animal and plant life along
the way.
    ISBN  1-57103-205-3
    1. Hiking—Juvenile literature. [1. Hiking.]  I. Title II. Series:
Armentrout, David. 1962-  Outdoor adventures.
GV199.5.A72  1998
796.51—dc21                                          98–18418
                                                          CIP
                                                          AC

**Printed in the USA**

# TABLE OF CONTENTS

# HIKING

If you have been on a long walk on a park trail, then you have been on a hike. Hiking means walking for a long time. It is an activity that almost anyone can do.

People hike for the pleasure of being outdoors, for exercise, and even for relaxation.

Hiking is a great way to explore nature. Some hikers take short, easy walks on hard, smooth trails, while other hikers enjoy long walks on rough, hilly **terrain** (tuh RAYN).

Sometimes hikers go on overnight trips. Overnight hiking is called backpacking. A backpack holds supplies needed for a hike and an overnight stay outdoors.

*Always hike with another person.*

5

# PLANNING A HIKE

Many beautiful trails can be found in every state. Travel guides list a large number of popular hiking areas.

There are trails that meet all skill levels. Beginners should stay on well-marked trails. These trails are safe, require little climbing, and often lead to the best-liked areas of a park.

*Most trails have a trail map and local rules posted.*

*Day hikes are good exercise and a great way to see animals.*

Trail maps are usually available. Also, dress for the weather and take drinking water with you.

Tell someone at home where you are going to hike and what time you expect to return. If it gets late and you are lost, a search team will know where to look for you.

# CLOTHING

Wearing the right kind of clothing and footwear is very important. Good hiking boots or shoes are most important. Make sure you pick boots or shoes that fit well. Boots that are too big or too small will cause sore feet.

Wear clothes made of wool or man-made materials, such as **nylon** (NY lahn). They keep you warm and dry. Wear your clothing in layers. Pieces can be added or removed as you warm up or cool down. Always be prepared for rain. A rain **poncho** (PAHN choh) folds up and can be packed away easily.

*When going on long hikes, remember to take rain gear.*

# SUPPLIES

The longer your hike the more you will need to carry with you. Some basic supplies should be carried on every hike. The supplies can be carried in a daypack. For longer, overnight trips, you will need a backpack.

The well-prepared day hiker should carry a first-aid kit, water, snacks, rain gear, map, and **compass** (KUM pus).

Backpackers will take extra gear, such as a tent, sleeping bag, flashlight, matches, small gas stove, and food and water.

*Overnight hikes require carrying food, spare clothing, and other gear.*

# TRAIL FOOD

Hiking is exercise. It takes a lot of energy to walk up and down long, hilly trails. Most people eat three meals a day. To keep your energy up when hiking, you may need to eat more often.

*You should always carry water if your hike is longer than two hours.*

*These kids rest while enjoying a snack.*

Hikers who go on long trips like to carry light foods that are easy to prepare. Nuts and dried fruits are good for you and make great trail snacks. Don't forget to take plenty of drinking water with you.

# SAFETY AND FIRST AID

Safety should come first when hiking. Everyone should stay on marked trails and not hike too far in one day.

Even experienced hikers fall and get injured. It is very important to watch where you walk. It is easy to trip on a tree root or log. Be extra careful when hiking on trails that take you along a cliff or fast-moving water.

A hiker's first-aid kit should include cloth and creams to clean and dress a cut, tweezers, pain relievers, accident rescue information, and money for a telephone call.

*Sore feet are common when hiking. Always wear comfortable shoes on the trail.*

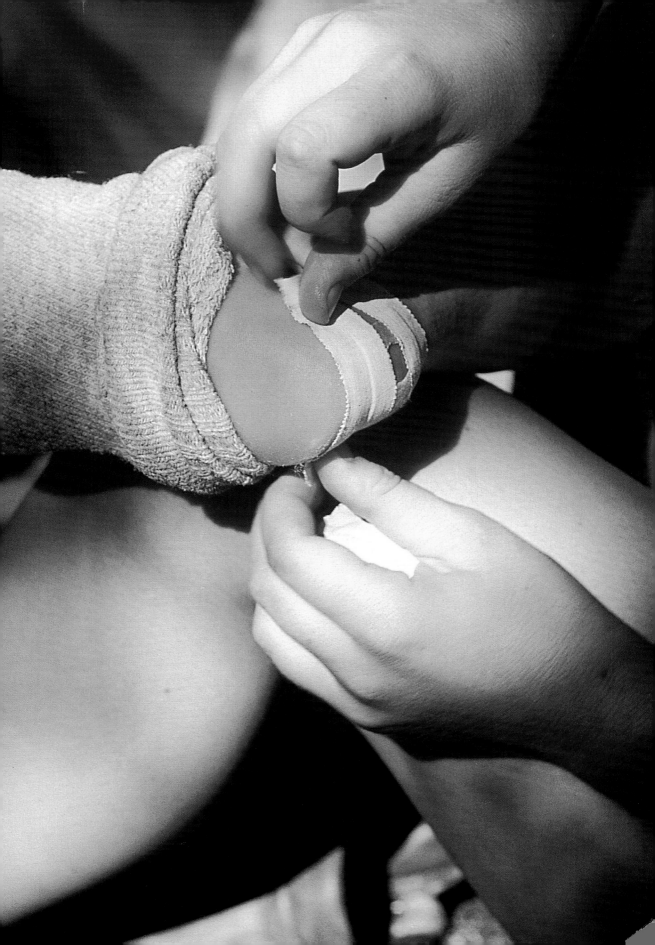

# ANIMAL LIFE

Seeing animals in their natural **environment** (en VY run ment) is one of the great joys of hiking. You may see some animals along the trail, although most animals try to avoid people.

Remember that you are not at a zoo, and wild animals can be unsafe. Be sure to keep a safe distance from large animals such as deer, bears, and moose. Some small animals, like snakes, can also be a danger. Most snakes are not **poisonous** (POY zuh nus), but you should avoid them.

*Hiking is a great way to see wildlife.*

# PLANT LIFE

You see a mix of plants when hiking. Many people hike just because they enjoy the flowering trees and plants along the trails.

You know to be careful around animals, but did you know that plants can be risky too? Some wild plants are **edible** (ED uh bul), but some can make you sick if eaten.

*Learning about the plants in the wild is a good idea, as some plants are poisonous.*

*Sometimes fallen trees block a trail.*

A more common risk is the **allergic reaction** (uh LER jik  ree AK shun) you can get from brushing against certain plants. Poison ivy and poison oak can cause the skin to itch. From books you can learn to recognize these plants so that you can avoid them.

# LEAVE ONLY YOUR FOOTPRINTS

Hiking is a very popular activity. Hikers crowd the most popular trails during the spring and summer months. If every one of these hikers carelessly dropped a candy wrapper, the trail would quickly lose its natural beauty.

It is important to respect the trail and other hikers. A smart hiker once said, "Leave only footprints, take only memories." Today, most hikers try to follow that simple rule.

*Hiking can be as simple as you like.*

# GLOSSARY

**allergic reaction** (uh LER jik  ree AK shun) —
reacting to certain foods, plants, or other matter
with sneezing, coughing and the like

**compass** (KUM pus) — a device that shows
direction

**edible** (ED uh bul) — safe to be eaten

**environment** (en VY run ment) — surroundings

**nylon** (NY lahn) — a strong elastic man-made
material used to make cloth, yarn, and plastics

**poisonous** (POY zuh nus) — a substance that can
injure or kill

**poncho** (PAHN choh) — a waterproof jacket that
slips on over the head

**terrain** (tuh RAYN) — the ground surface

*There are many beautiful places waiting for you to explore.*

# INDEX

FURTHER READING

Find out more about Outdoor Adventures with these helpful books:

DuFresne, Jim. *Outdoor Adventures With Children.* The Mountaineers, 1990.

Logue, Victoria; Logue, Frank; and Carroll, Mark. *Kids Outdoors/Skills and Knowledge for Outdoor Adventures.* Ragged Mountain Press, 1996.

Strauss, Robert. *Adventure Trekking/A Handbook for Independent Travelers.* The Mountaineers, 1996.